Occult

S U N · S I G N

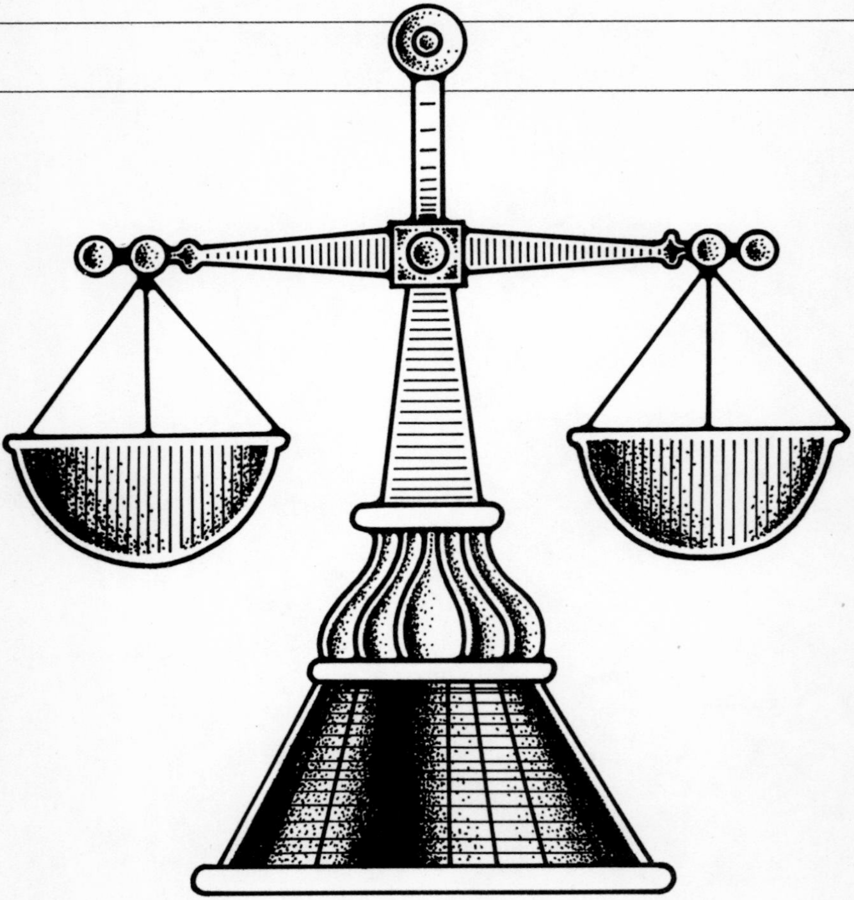

♎ ♎ ♎ ♎ ♎

SUN · SIGN

LIBRA

by james a. lely

creative education

childrens press

Published by Creative Education, Inc., 123 South Broad Street, Mankato, Minnesota 56001 Copyright © 1978 by Creative Education, Inc. International copyrights reserved in all countries. No part of this book may be reproduced in any form without written permission from the publisher. Printed in the United States.

Distributed by Childrens Press, 1224 West Van Buren Street, Chicago, Illinois 60607

Library of Congress Cataloging in Publication Data

Lely, James A
  Libra.

  SUMMARY: Details the personality traits, physical appearance, and other characteristics of individuals born between September 23 and October 23. Lists famous people born under the sign of Libra.
  1. Libra (Astrology)—Juvenile literature. [1. Libra (Astrology) 2. Astrology] I. Title.
BF1727.45.L44   133.5'4   77-12239
ISBN 0-87191-647-9

SUN · SIGN

LIBRA

contents

your sun sign is libra

If your birthday is between
September 23 and October 23,
your sun sign is Libra.
Your key phrase is "I balance."
Your planet is Venus.
Your element is air.
Your symbol is the Scale.
Your energy is cardinal.
Your color is blue.
Your metal is copper.
Your gems are diamond and opal.
Your flower is the violet.

You are the half-way point
in the zodiac.
You represent
balance, justice, and equilibrium.
A pure Libran possesses
the ability to see
all sides of any question.

7

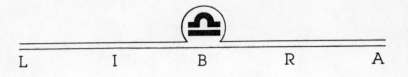
To you, more than to any other sign,
justice is all important.
You cannot be swayed by mere emotion.
You can see
what will be
the long-range result of any decision.
You take time to weigh
every bit of information
about any matter
before acting or suggesting.

Your chief fault
may be your inability
to decide anything quickly.
As a Libra you may never develop
a set of principles
or beliefs
which can help you
be consistent and quick
in handling your day-to-day affairs.

8

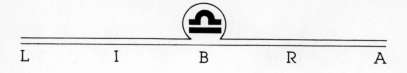

A Libra should practice
quickly sorting important information
from non-essential details
and then act without
too many second thoughts.
In spending too much time
deciding whether or not to take
a bus or a train,
you may miss both.

Libra is gifted
with wonderful powers of perception.
You can seemingly absorb details
right out of the air.
You instinctively know much
about strangers
as well as your friends
and you have great compassion.

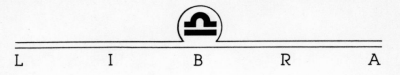

Libras can easily identify
with almost anyone.
They know that beneath the frown
of the person sitting next to them
in school
lives an ordinary person
who has the same
problems, delights,
fears, and hopes as they do.

You are charming and gentle
and draw many people to you.
You are tolerant of people
and their various ways of living.
You are as comfortable
with someone who is conservative
and who would never think of
running in public
as you are with
those who are rowdy
and dress in brilliant colors.

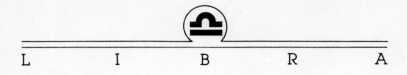

You are free from prejudices.
For a Libra never "pre-judges."
Instead, a Libra always looks
at everything and everyone
as if for the first time.

Libran judgements are based on the merits
of the situation.
You don't care if your friends
are old or young or in between.
You like people
and aren't too interested
in how many birthdays
they've celebrated.
A Libra is rarely troubled
by differences in race.
Your friend's skin could be lavender
and you would probably comment
on how well his complexion looks
against his brown shirt.

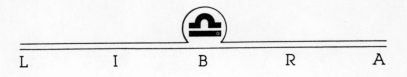

L   I   B   R   A

Because you are an air sign,
your voice is probably quiet.
You may never become an opera singer
unless your horoscope
has other influences in it—
but you will always love
to sing and to listen to singing.
Venus is the planet of beauty
and because it rules Libra,
you have a strong appreciation
of beauty and the arts.

You may not be able to decide
what color to paint your room,
but the four colors you finally choose
will go well with each other.
You insist on harmony.
One of your main gifts
is the ability to encourage others
to appreciate
a sense of beauty and harmony.
You are anxious
to share with the world
your pleased and balanced view of it.

12

L I B R A

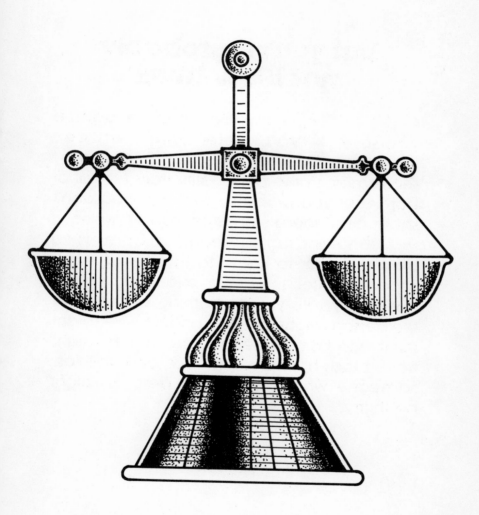

13

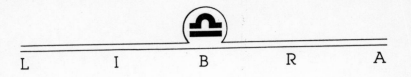

but you're probably not 100% libra

Do you recognize yourself? If you were born between September '23 and October 23, you may share most of the personality traits typical of Libra. But you probably feel that you don't share all of them. This is not too surprising.

Knowing that someone is a Gemini or a Libra is similar to knowing that he or she is Japanese, Italian, or Egyptian. A person's nationality tells you something about what the person might look like and how he might think and act. Someone who is Irish might have black hair, a round face and freckles. Someone who is of Scottish descent might be thrifty.

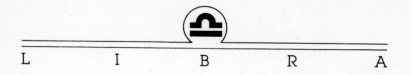

Yet knowing a person's nationality won't tell you everything. Not all people of the same nationality share the same traits. To get a clearer picture of the person, you would have to find out about the person's age, sex, religion, favorite sport and hobbies.

In the same way, a person's sun sign can provide some general information. But it cannot reveal all of the aspects of a personality. If an astrologer wanted to know more about a person, he or she would have to find out exactly when and where the person was born. Then the astrologer would calculate the exact position of the sun, the moon and the planets of our solar system in relation to the earth at the moment of the person's birth.

Astrologers believe that human beings are affected by the same energies that cause the sun, the moon and the planets to move in their orbits. They believe that a chart showing the position of these heavenly bodies at the moment of birth can be a kind of blueprint giving clues to a person's personality and potential.

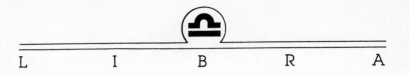
But drawing up such a chart is no easy matter, since the earth, as well as the sun, moon and planets, are all constantly in motion. Because of this movement, even identical twins born only minutes apart will have slightly different birth charts, and two Librans whose birthdays are ten days apart can be very different indeed.

Interpreting a birth chart is even more complicated than constructing it. That's why many astrologers advise beginners to start their study of astrology by learning about sun signs. Since the sun affects life on the earth more than the other stars and planets do, the sun sign is a very important factor in a birth chart. Just remember that it's not the only factor.

One more word of caution: it takes approximately 29 days for the sun to move through each of the twelve zones or sun signs of the zodiac. But the exact time when the sun passes from one zone to the next varies from year to year, so the dates listed for any sun sign are only approximate.

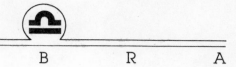

If you were born on September 23, you might be either Libra or Virgo, or if your birthday is October 23, your sun sign could be Libra or Scorpio. In order to tell for sure which you are, you would have to consult an astrological reference book called an ephemeris. After making certain corrections depending on precisely where you were born, you would have to look up your exact time of birth in order to see whether the sun had changed signs by then.

If you were born at one of these turning points and don't have access to an ephemeris, try reading about both signs. See if you can tell which description fits you better.

Your sun sign can't tell you everything about yourself. But it can give some general characteristics. In reading about your sun sign you may come to know and understand yourself better.

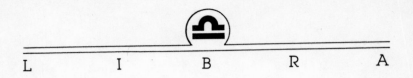

what you may look like

Your sun sign affects your physical appearance, as well as your personality. Just remember that there are other factors at work and that you probably won't look exactly like this Libran portrait.

A typical Libra may have:
— dimples, either on the chin, cheeks, or knees
— a generally pleasant expression
— a bow-shaped mouth
— a soft, gentle smile
— curves, rather than angles, throughout the body and face
— a clear and easy laugh
— deep-set eyes which are in turn merry and distant

— fine but thick hair
— hands that are neither long nor short, fat nor thin, very much the balance among all types of hands
— even proportions throughout the body

Unlike many other signs, Libras are not generally known for any specific type of appearance. Like the harmonious Libra mind, there are usually brief displays of various extremes. When a Libra is feeling lazy or bored, the body responds accordingly, giving the impression that the person is a slack, loose package. But when the same Libra swings back to the other side of the scales, the body reflects all of the nervous energy common to the air signs.

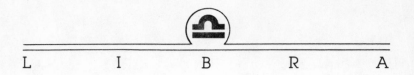

L   I   B   R   A

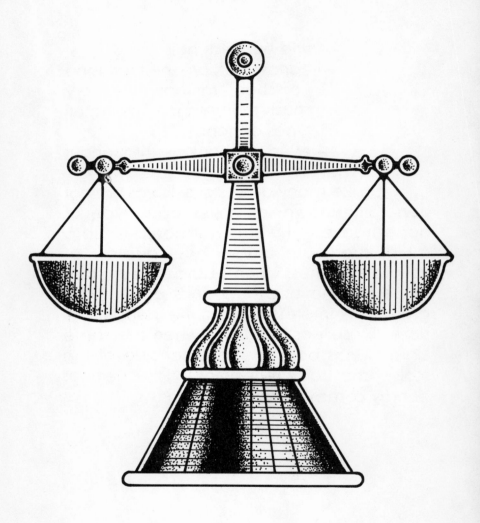

20

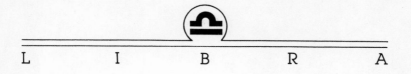

what you might expect

Your sun sign also affects the way you think and act. As you read the following descriptions of how a Libra might act in certain situations, see if you can recognize yourself. But remember that this is a hypothetical person. Don't look for a mirror image of yourself. You will probably only catch glimpses of the you you know.

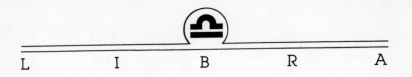
school

A Libra always wants all the facts and you will take special delight in your history class. You want to know how other people have reached their decisions and made their judgements. That way you are better equipped to make your own.

You favorite classes will probably be music, speech, theater, debate, journalism, and maybe a chemistry class. You may never learn how to read music but you were born with a good ear and can tell instantly who is off-key. You have a natural talent for harmonizing in music. Even though your voice may not be the strongest one in the chorus, it may have a deep and full quality when you feel especially emotional about the music you are singing.

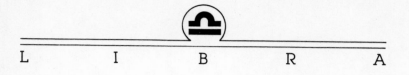
You insist on people getting along with each other. Through entertaining speeches, or as a moderator in a debate, you will do your best to persuade warring factions to bury the hatchet. As editor or contributor to your school paper, you will continue your campaign to spread good will throughout the school. If the students and the administration are at odds over an issue, you will calmly write articles which clearly explain the position of both sides—and then you will suggest a solution. Because you are frequently approached for advice on a wide range of subjects, you may decide to write a column on advice to the lovelorn, or a social column with suggestions for great parties.

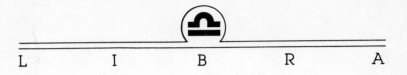

L I B R A

Your involvement in theater will run the range from serious drama to skits you wrote yourself on fund raising for the Christmas dance. You are a born organizer: you could persuade Tom Sawyer to paint his own fence, and he'd thank you for the opportunity. If you are starring in a show, you aren't content to just sit around the stage door waiting for people to ask for your autograph. You will be all over town before opening night, distributing posters and spreading good will until everyone knows that something big is going to happen. People who haven't the slightest interest in theater will be persuaded to spend long nights painting sets and building costumes—and you'll see that they have a good time while doing it!

Libra's energy is cardinal, which means that you are the one most likely to start projects and to inspire enthusiasm over your ideas. In chemistry class you'll be anxious to begin each experiment, and you may take

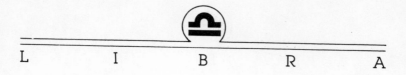

on more lab work than is required. You will lose interest, though, when the experiment is over and it's time to go back to the classroom to do the mathematics which explain the experiment. You quickly become bored with details and you will start to look elsewhere for a new project.

As a Libra you probably will go to college because you have a great thirst for knowledge. Besides, as president of your sorority or fraternity, you'll stir up more fun and excitement than has been present in those hallowed halls for years. You may change your major several times, and in the end, may decide not to finish school at all. Libras have a hard time deciding what is right for them. If you think that you can learn more outside school, you'll leave in an instant. It doesn't seem to do you much harm, but a Libra can rarely finish any project.

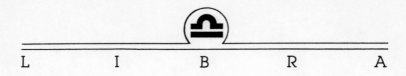

travel

You like to take off on a trip on short notice and with no preparation. If you only have time to throw some clothes into a suitcase and rush to the airport, you feel things are going according to schedule. You prefer to travel in the company of a friend but rarely enjoy going with a large group. At your destination, you will prefer to examine whatever catches your eye. You will normally not be interested in a formal bus tour of a city. Your favorite way to travel is by car, for you like to examine all the people and sights along the way. You love to gaze at the countryside as much as you enjoy a crowded restaurant in the heart of a city.

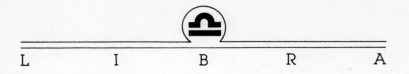

L   I   B   R   A

Your main objective on any trip is to get a sense of the history of your country. The site of a great battle, an inn untouched by time, a hex symbol on a barn, a ghost town-all will start your imagination working on how people used to live and think. You have a keen sense of the continuity of history. You are constantly finding similarities between the way things were and the way we do things now. You'll return home full of anecdotes about what you've seen. You will be better equipped than ever to explain to your friends that today's problems are no greater than those of the past.

27

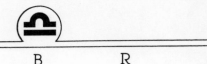

moving

You hate it. A Libra is a homebody of the first degree, and you settle your roots deep into the ground you call your own. A Libra needs one space where nothing changes, a place of rest and quiet. You've agonized over every detail of decorating your house or room, and it suits you perfectly. You may leave a room undecorated for years simply because you haven't found the right pieces for it. Your indecisiveness is always reflected in your surroundings. You would not be happy if your parent or spouse were in a job which required frequent transfers. You like your neighbors and you like the scratch in the paint on your cupboards which you have been meaning to fix for the last two years.

However, if the worst is inevitable and you must move, you will simply grin and bear it. A Libra is not a complainer and realizes that something good can be made of anything—no matter how unpleasant!

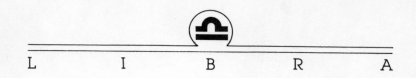

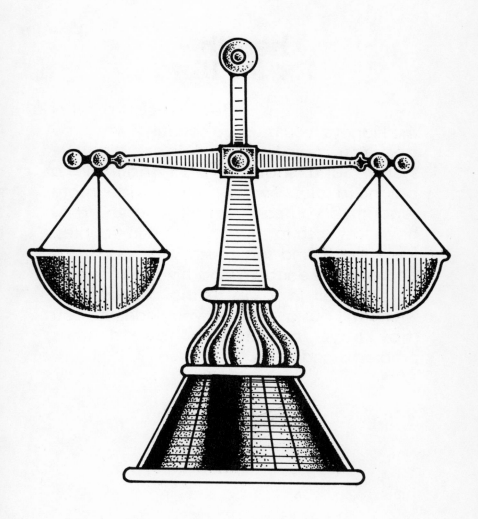

29

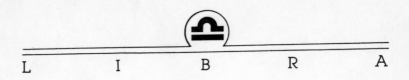

health – Rx for libra

Because Libra rules the kidneys, you must be careful of what you eat. You may have a delicate digestive system and should try to maintain a balanced diet. Sweets will provide more sugar than you can burn off, and you may have to watch for obesity and skin troubles. Spicy foods and too much soda pop may encourage heartburn and hives. Emotional upsets result in toxins in the bloodstream which will put a strain on your kidneys. You may have a tendency toward sinus problems and colds.

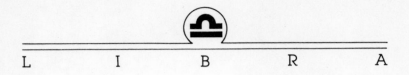

If you don't get enough rest, you will become irritable and your thinking will be unclear. To keep yourself in good health, you must maintain an orderly schedule of eating and rest. If you become ill, the best cure is more rest in a quiet, pleasant room, perhaps with some soothing music. You should avoid unpleasant scenes.

The very nature of Libra, which is moving from one end of the scales to the other, tends to be harmful to your health. It is important to be aware of internal elements that are bound to be troublesome and to strive to practice control and moderation in your habits.

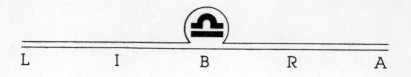

other libras like you

Some of your Libra traits will be more noticeable when you're young. Others will become apparent as you grow older. Some traits will be especially evident in certain roles or occupations. See if you can identify typical Libran characteristics in other Libras you may know.

L   I   B   R   A

if your
best friend
is a libra

You spend a lot of time in your Libra friend's basement. Her recreation room is a perfect place for the many parties she likes to give. If there's a disagreement among your friends, this Libra feels that a relaxed social gathering is the best arena in which to work out differences. And there's never a dull moment at those parties, either. A record player is always playing just the right music and everyone dances. The refreshments are unusual and very tasty. Soon, any differences are completely forgotten, and everyone is happy again.

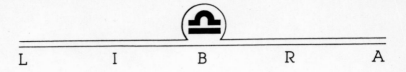

Just knowing that you are the best friend of a Libra tells you plenty about yourself. Your Libra friend expects certain things of his or her friends. You are expected to be full of the joy of life. You probably have lots of energy, a quick and intelligent mind, and you are interested in anything and everything. You and your friends share some interests even though your chief work or interests may be different.

A Libra expects honesty from a friend and is always honest and reliable in return. When you have an appointment to meet at the malt shop, you'd better be on time. Your friend will wait for you once or twice. But if you are frequently late you will have to start looking for a new pal. A Libra expects you to show consideration in your relationship. Your Libra friend may be an eager photographer. You'd better start running if you happen to put a fingerprint on the lens of her camera!

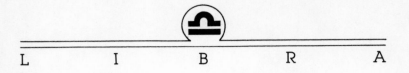
A Libra can't stand carelessness and never is guilty of spilling milk on a new shirt or accidentally breaking a dish. Because your friend always thinks before acting, she expects that everyone else will follow suit. That may be intolerent, but the rewards for following those wishes are great. If you have a problem with anything—from studying to skateboarding—your Libra friend is right at hand to offer helpful advice.

A Libra has friends who have varied interests. Sometimes those interests are so different that two people close to the Libra can't stand each other. The wise Libra, however, will work until a happy meeting ground can be found. A Libra's world will always have harmony!

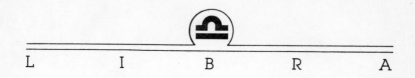

L   I   B   R   A

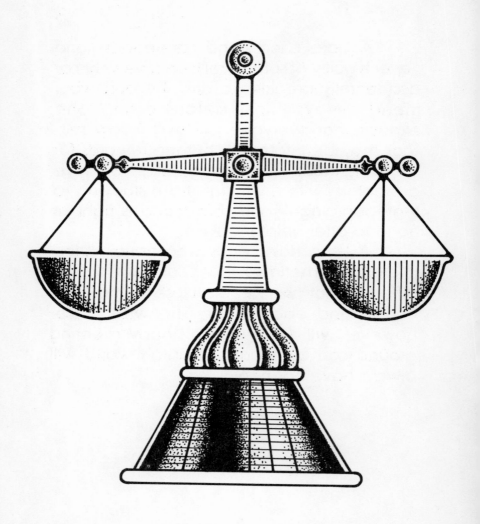

36

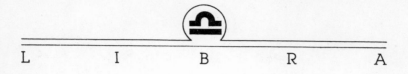

if your
mother is a libra

By now, you've grown used to having fish and spaghetti at the same meal. Your Libra mother probably spent a good hour trying to decide on a main course and ended up serving both. Your fork and knife will be of different patterns, too. It's not that Libras are unconscious of the differences, it's just that both patterns looked beautiful and so they were both selected.

Your home is a restful retreat. You would be scandalized by any sign of quarreling in the house because your Libra mother firmly believes that harmony and peace are the keys to successful family life.

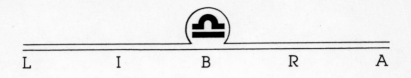

By no means, however, does that mean that your home will seem like a cave which hasn't been visited for decades. On the contrary, you are never surprised to wake up in the morning to discover that three or four out-of-town friends decided to stop off and visit. There's always an extra bed or couch for a friend who might have a good story to tell. Your friends are always welcome in your home, and they may turn out to be better friends with your mother than with you. After all, she was born understanding people and their needs.

Your mother goes from one extreme to the other—just like clockwork. Although she can't stand a disorderly house, she may ignore it for weeks, preferring to lounge around reading a magazine. When the pendulum starts to swing back, though, that

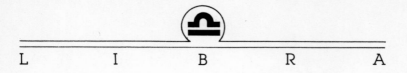

house will sparkle just in time for the guests to arrive. Without batting an eyelash, your mother will have arranged a party for one hundred and fifty guests. Before the night is over, they will be arranging a parade complete with bagpipe players, to entertain the neighborhood. Your mother lives life to the fullest!

Your Libra mother is deadly honest, and she expects the same of you. It is wise for you to remember that Aries is opposite Libra in the zodiac, and Aries lends to Libra its keen sense of smell. Whether the offending smell happens to be your laundry, which has been piling up for a month, or some untimely smoke on your breath, you are better off not trying to deny anything. A Libra mother is consistent, and you always know what to expect.

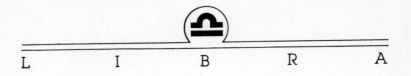

if your younger brother is a libra

You may have the only garage on the block which doubles as a theater. Last week your kid brother wrote, organized, directed, and naturally, starred in a gala production. It drew a good audience, as well! He usually has several projects going. He and a friend have organized a lending library in your basement. On the side, your brother sells comic books.

Last summer, he gathered up his many friends, stuffed an old gunny sack and found some rope to make a long swing over the river. All were welcome as long as fun was the goal. Your Libra brother loves to ride horses bareback—typical of his delight in

outdoor activities. He's always off making up and organizing games with other boys and girls in the neighborhood. When they finish playing, they retreat for a glass of lemonade in the clubhouse he built.

Your brother loves swimming and biking, and if there's a deserted warehouse in town, your parents will have a hard time convincing him to stay away from it. If he does stray from the straight and narrow path, he is the first to admit it.

Even at his young age, he is a diplomat and can break up a dog fight as easily as he can decide the fairest schedule for washing dishes.

Despite the fact that it is not ordinary for sisters and brothers to get along all the time, you regret that you can't spend more time with him.

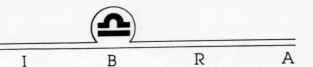

libra careers

The Libran job in life is to spread harmony, peace, and beauty throughout the world—even if the world for you is limited to your community. You like a clean and pleasant work atmosphere, and you could bring a sense of order to a coal mine. Libras usually have trouble in jobs where quick decisions are needed. Even intense pressure won't push you to hurry your answers—you always need to look carefully at all sides of a question.

There are many careers where the kind of impartial, thoughtful analysis is useful. The most obvious career is law. Whether as a lawyer or as a judge, you will listen carefully to the cases of the plaintiff and the defendant. You will then go off to study the proceedings of countless similar cases which have been heard before. Your decisions will

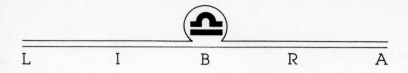

combine the requirements of the law, your own sense of justice, and the wisdom of others who have had to make the same decisions. You are never hasty in your judgements; you have a keen awareness of what your words will mean to everyone involved in the trial.

Diplomacy is another obvious choice for Libra. As a career, diplomacy goes beyond the mere tactfulness you use when talking to your friends or teachers. The jobs or even the lives of many may be affected by how clearly you can understand your position and the position of your opponent. You have an intuitive ability to understand that a person can say one thing and mean another. It is your job to correctly interpret what that other meaning is. When you think that you understand the motives of both parties, you try to find a solution which will make everyone happy.

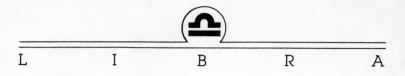

Diplomacy is a broad field. Representing your country in a meeting with another country is only one facet of the field. After all, the job of Secretary of State isn't open for applications very often. All areas of politics call for diplomats. Elected officials represent the needs and wants of the electorate to a group of people who control the money or power.

As a Libra, you may become a salesman. You will then try to persuade people that your company's product is something that they can't live without. In doing this, you must have the ability to understand the life and situation of your potential customer. Libras usually know what someone wants to hear. It is not in your nature to cheat anyone, and you wouldn't sell a worthless item. Thus you always leave a trail of people who are happy to have dealt with you.

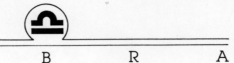
Your love of beauty and your capacity for details may lead you toward a career in the design field. You may turn toward architecture, graphic design, interior decorating, or gardening. Your ability to understand the problems of others may turn you toward counseling or the ministry. Libras make fine actors and actresses because they can "become" whatever character they are playing. You know what people are all about and can be totally sympathetic in your portrayals of them.

You may choose to go into advertising or science. You do not pre-judge anything, are always open to new information and ideas, and can fairly compare them to old ideas. As a nurse or physician, you are second only to Cancer as a natural in the caring professions.

L I B R A

famous people born under the sign of libra

Julie Andrews, actress
Sarah Bernhardt, actress
Charles Boyer, actor
Truman Capote, writer
Jimmy Carter, U.S. President
Dwight Eisenhower, U.S. President
T.S. Eliot, writer
John K. Galbraith, economist

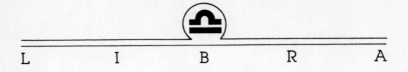

L   I   B   R   A

Mahatma Gandhi, spiritual and political
    leader
George Gershwin, composer
Charlton Heston, actor
Rev. Jesse Jackson, civil rights leader
John Lennon, composer, singer
Franz Liszt, composer
Mickey Mantle, baseball player
Nietzsche, philosopher
Eleanor Roosevelt, humanist
Ed Sullivan, master of ceremonies
Oscar Wilde, writer
Noah Webster, statesman

sun signs

for

young

people

creative education

ARIES ● March 21 — April 20
TAURUS ● April 20 — May 21
GEMINI ● May 21 — June 21
CANCER ● June 21 — July 23
LEO ● July 23 — August 23
VIRGO ● August 24 — September 23
LIBRA ● September 23 — October 23
SCORPIO ● October 23 — November 22
SAGITTARIUS ● November 22 — December 22
CAPRICORN ● December 22 — January 20
AQUARIUS ● January 20 — February 18
PISCES ● February 18 — March 20